GROW
YOUR
DIGITAL
AGENCY

How to run a successful digital agency
- a simple method

Robert Craven

Grow Your Digital Agency

For Cal, Jessie, Bonnie and Ben

THE DIRECTORS' CENTRE LTD
1 The High Street, Woolley, Bath, BA1 8AR
Tel: +44 (0) 1225 851 044
Email: ty@directorscentre.com
Website: www.directorscentre.com

First published in Great Britain in 2015

What Others Say

"Robert Craven says that 'your whole business hinges on what your customer gets from you'. I wholeheartedly agree."
Sir Richard Branson

"Having built two agencies, I think this book is crammed full of great advice. Everyone should 'score their business' AND use the Profit Improvement Checklist."
David Gilroy, Conscious Solutions

"I wholeheartedly commend this book. I promise you that it is full of practical, implementable wisdom."
Prof Malcolm McDonald, Cranfield School of Management

"Cuts through all the flummery so common in books of this type to get to what's necessary to make an agency grow in terms of customers, costs and strategy. Recommended."
Guy Clapperton, Author, "This Is Social Media"

"For owners of digital marketing agencies, this book will provide a short, sharp burst of reality; opening your eyes to where your agency is falling short in the three key areas."
Veronica Pullen, Word of Mouth Local Social Marketing

Grow Your Digital Agency

"GYDA breaks down exactly what you need to do to get the growth you want. If you follow the step-by-step guidance in this highly practical book then success will be guaranteed."
Simon Hazeldine, Author, "Neuro-Sell: How Neuroscience Can Power Your Sales Success"

"Wish I'd read something like this at my first agency. Good, simple advice – yet really quite sophisticated at the same time! I learnt the hard way – you just need to read this!"
David Coe, CEO, oe:gen limited

"An essential guide for digital agencies to ensure their business succeeds and grows. Easy to read, packed with examples."
Graham Jones, Internet Psychologist

"If you want to scale, I recommend you take the time to read and apply Robert's wisdom."
Krishna De, Digital Communications Strategist

"There's something for everyone. The dashboard tracking element was spot on."
Karen Reyburn, Managing Director, The Profitable Firm

"As a 30-person agency we thought we knew a thing or two about running a business; this book is full of wisdom."
Guy Levine, CEO, Return on Digital

Grow Your Digital Agency

"A 'must have' for anyone running a digital agency. It is challenging but entirely practical."
Tony Robinson OBE, Co-Founder, Enterprise Rockers

"A practical, bold, easy-to-understand and 'ready to be applied immediately' guide to grow your digital agency from zero to hero."
Adrian Niculescu, C Level Marketing

"Do read it. And then re-read it every six months."
Sofie Sandell, Author, "Digital Leadership"

Contents

Foreword

A large part of my role at Google is ensuring that digital agencies are successful so that they can better support small and large businesses in their digital journey.

Running an agency, like any other business, is very rewarding, but also fraught with challenges. Cash flow, recruitment, winning new business and payroll can keep an agency owner working 7 days a week. Often, the sole focus is ensuring that the business maintains itself as a going concern in terms of cash.

I first met Robert at a business event in Huntingdon, and he impressed me with his ability to make an instant connection with the audience. It was hard not to be engaged as Robert worked the room, and pretty soon everyone was smiling in agreement and taking notes.

In this book, Robert has managed to provide a framework for the busy agency CEO or partner, in an easily digestible format. In addition, he asks some tough questions - "What is your goal?", "Why are you doing this?" and "How can you plan your journey so that it is ultimately successful?"

Raja Saggi
Head of B2B Marketing
Google UK

Grow Your Digital Agency

Introduction

*"A book for digital agencies. You cannot be serious?
Why digital agencies? Why now?"*

My client, MD of a fast growing agency, had a great point.

Of course he missed the irony. He said this after a two-hour heated discussion sorting out how and why running his agency seemed to be getting harder and harder and not easier and easier.

There are a hundred reasons why this book is not necessary but way more reasons why it is.

WHY DIGITAL AGENCIES?

I am using a broad definition of a 'digital agency', that is a firm that handles all things digital. Specifically, they might have expertise in the strategy or the tactics of any of:

- Website design and development
- Blogging/content creation
- Email marketing
- Social media
- Search Engine Marketing (SEM) and Search Engine Optimisation (SEO)
- Marketing automation

3

- Analytics
- Online advertising.

Digital agencies and their people are great at doing their job and there is no shortage of advice, support and learning on the 'doing the doing' bit.

However, it is apparent that many agencies (whether they be hybrids, PR, SEO, content, advertising or web-focused) are lacking basic 'business growing' skills:
- Business strategy and planning
- Winning business: sales and marketing
- Managing people and operations.

Most are not expert in these fields because they are expert do-ers not expert business growers.

The premise of this book is simple: a better understanding of how to grow a business will help you to run a better and more profitable agency.

WHAT SIZE AGENCY?

This book is squarely aimed at privately-owned agencies although the principles apply whatever the size of the business. It will be of particular relevance to agencies at transition or inflection points.

Typically these are roughly at 5 staff, 10-20 staff and 40-60 staff where new ways of working are required to accommodate the change in scales, scope and style of the business.

At each stage, the owner-director and the business need to move to a different style of management. Either that or stagnate and lose direction. The clue is in statements like:

> *"I seem to be working harder now even though the business is so much bigger. Surely it doesn't have to be this way!"*

My reply is the often quoted phrase:

> *"What got you here won't get you there."*
> [Marshall Goldsmith]

Specifically, I have written this book with several people in mind as the target audience – real people and real businesses I have worked with (names changed to protect the innocent – but I think they know who they are):

- Lisa, MD, 100-person, 'Integrated Comms Agency'
- James, MD, 25-person 'Digital Design Agency'
- Tim, Creative Director, 15-person 'Creative Digital Design Agency'
- Sam, DX Director/Owner, 5-person, 'Digital Strategy Agency'.

(Fascinating how agencies describe themselves and whether clients know what they really mean!)

WHAT THIS BOOK IS NOT

This book:
- offers no magic formula or silver bullet promising to transform your business in three simple steps
- will not make the tough decisions for you and will not do the work for you
- is not about code, Adwords, algorithms or anything digital. That is your area of excellence; my area is growing your agency business.

WHAT THIS BOOK WILL DO

This book will:
- share the tools, tips and techniques that the above-average performers use to grow their agencies
- show you how and what other digital agencies have done to take their business to the next level
- be short, sharp and to the point. A waffle-free zone.

THE 'OLOGY'

The thinking behind this book has been as follows:
- "Keep it simple but powerful"
  I am writing for people who want to get to the point
- "Stuff that works"
  Share what has worked in other agencies and businesses.

I have tried to write in plain English and keep away from too much tech-savvy language.

So, if you want a short, simple book that shows you how to run a more successful digital agency then you are in the right place.

The tools, tips and techniques in this book have been applied to, or learnt from, working with marketing and digital agencies and their owners: agencies I advise, consult or (have) run myself.

I guarantee that this book is free of business school nonsense but is full of tools that work to grow your digital agency.

I call it:
> *"stuff that works."*

The problem most agencies have is that they are great at the digital piece but not so great at the 'growing a business' piece. To successfully grow an agency requires some discipline and structured thinking, a roadmap.

Hope is not a method.

Robert Craven   Bath, May 2015

A Sense Of Logic

We spend too much time working *in* the business, dealing with the granular minutiae of keeping the business going. We do not spend enough time *on* the business: designing, planning and mapping out the future.

That is what working with over 100 digital agencies tells me.

And when we do try to start working *on* the business, we usually start in the wrong place, simply reacting to the latest crisis, be it people, customers or cash.

WORKING FROM THE BIG PICTURE DOWN

Stepping back from the business makes us realise that we can be busy fools, madly chasing our tails but not sure if we are being busy at what is really important. Not sure if we even know what really is important.

There seems to be a logical hierarchy for planning a business. In fact the hierarchy isn't that different from the design process in a digital agency.

While you could start anywhere, there is an attractive logic and simplicity about starting at the top with the big picture and working down to the detail in the following order:

1. Business strategy and planning.
2. Winning business: sales and marketing.
3. Managing operations.
4. Teams, people and relationships.

Most agencies literally try to build their business from the bottom up trying to find a business model that fits their existing people and skills. This may be a little short-sighted especially if you end up positioning yourself in an undifferentiated and over-crowded market or one where there is little demand.

TIME FOR SOME DEFINITIONS

1. Strategy
> *"planning while being aware of the outside environment"*

2. Marketing
> *"why and how...we get which people...to buy what from us..."*

3. Operations
> *"doing the doing"*

Systems, processes to deliver our product/service.

4. People

"the backbone of the business"

Your relationships, internally (as leader) and externally (as representative of the firm), are crucial.

Before Anything: Mindset

For me, the key issue is mindset.

No amount of tools, techniques and strategies will work if you have the wrong mindset.

Too many agency creatives do not have the right mindset. They are too focused on working *in* the business or they are too preoccupied with petty political debates with clients or staff, or maybe they just don't think big enough. Others don't feel worthy, while others simply create a business around their own self-limiting beliefs.

WHICH AGENCY LEADER ARE YOU? (Burke et al)

- The **Strategist** gives their managers the tools to do the job, whilst they plan for the future
- The **Meddler** can't let go of routine tasks. The growth capacity of the firm is limited until they do let go: staff get hired but are not empowered and the boss doesn't make time to plan
- The **Hero** usually heads up operations, sales or design. They are the only person who really understands management policies and systems – so they often 'come to the rescue'

- The **Technician/Artisan** is typified by low management activity. Most of their time is spent delivering. They often remain 'one of the gang', with little authority. Future planning hardly happens.

SOME KEY QUESTIONS FOR YOU

- Have you got the skills to take the agency to the next level? Do you really want to?
- Are you building to sell or building to scale or building to create a legacy? Or just running an agency to pay the mortgage?
- Are you willing to make the tough decisions? If not, then why not?
- Is now the right time? If not now, then when?

STRATEGY...

In other words,

WHERE ARE YOU GOING?

The case for putting strategy at the head of the planning and organising hierarchy is simple. In the real world,

> *"If you don't know where you're going then any road will do."*
> [Cheshire Cat, Alice's Adventures in Wonderland]

We talk about strategy with clients but rarely succeed in doing our own strategy properly.

We attend badly run *'Strategy Awaydays'* which create plans we rarely deliver on; they have little to do with the day-to-day running of our agency. **But, it doesn't have to be that way.**

The *'Strategy Workshop'*, for want of a better phrase, is a simple yet powerful way to set up your agency for the coming year(s). It comprises of three apparently simple questions:

> *"Where are we now?"*
> *"Where are we going?"*
> *"How are we going to get there?"*

An additional question would be:

> *"How are we going to measure and monitor our performance to make sure we stay on track (or take the necessary evasive action)?"*

While it is not the remit of this deliberately slim volume to go into great detail, I would still like to cover off a few strategy basics. That's what we are going to cover next.

The Essence Of Strategy

We do need to be clear about what your strategy is. So, how do you answer the question,
> *"What is your strategy?"*

The essence, the DNA, of the strategy needs to be articulated in a short, succinct statement. One that everyone can understand.

Please, no nonsense platitudes like:
> *"maximise shareholder value by exceeding customer expectations while respecting the environment."*

SO, WHAT IS YOUR AGENCY'S STRATEGY?

For me your strategy is composed of three elements:

- **Objective(s)**
  This is a single precise statement that will drive the agency over the next three years or so
- **Scope**
  Encompasses the customer or service offering, the location and position in the market
- **Advantage**
  Sustainable competitive advantage (in other words, *'being different from or better than the rest and*

being able to maintain that position') is the essence of strategy, so it should be no surprise that advantage is the most critical aspect of a strategy statement and comprises:

    a)   your customer value proposition

    b)   your unique activities.

HOW THEN SHOULD AN AGENCY GO ABOUT CRAFTING ITS STRATEGY STATEMENT?

Strategy is planning while being aware of the outside environment.

The first step is an analysis of pressures and changes on the agency. Particular emphasis should be placed on customer and competitor analysis. (However, it is also worth considering pressures and changes in the world, industry, marketplace, competitors, customers, as well as changes in the Political, Economic Society, Technology, Legislative and Environmental landscape - also known as PESTLE).

The clever bit is to find a sweet spot where your capabilities (what you are good at) and the opportunities and demand match each other. Not so easy for an agency. However, just because it is difficult to do doesn't mean it shouldn't be done.

SAMPLE STRATEGY STATEMENTS (<40 words)

"To grow to 75 staff within three years offering bespoke, relevant digital services ("payment-by-results, digital marketing on a rope") to increase the profitability of mid-tier UK accounting practices with few IT/Web resources."

"To hit 25/25; 25/25k; 250/250* in 36m: working with M25-based medium-sized** service businesses needing customer acquisition campaigns to fuel their growth. Been-there-done-it marketing experts that deliver."

* 25% net profit with 25 people; 25 clients paying £25,000pa; 250 paying £250pm
**£5m-200m turnover

"Million turnover by Year 3; guru-led digital campaigns for edgy, young SW businesses needing more than just another full service agency. New best friend with a black book to die for."

We can argue about the wording but these examples give you a feel and a flavour.

ACTION

Write down your agency's strategy statement now, if you have one. If not, create one, a first draft.

THE KEY QUESTIONS TO ASK ABOUT YOUR STRATEGY

- *"What is your objective?"*
    What are you trying to achieve?
- *"What is your scope?"*
    What space are you working in?
- *"What is your advantage?"*
    What is your value proposition?
    What makes you unique?

How Good Is Your Agency?

This chapter introduces a framework that looks at your agency and its business performance. It is referred to by the acronym *FiMO – Finance, Marketing and Operations.*

FiMO is a framework which can be used to evaluate the strengths and weaknesses of your agency and to open up discussion to agree the 'state of play'.

Before you can look at future plans, your route map, you need to know how the agency is performing right now.

MEASURING AGENCY PERFORMANCE TO DATE

When asked:

> *'What measures should be used to assess your company's performance to date?'*

the same list of answers is usually put forward, give or take one or two differences. The list offered includes measures such as:

- turnover
- gross and net profit margin
- return on capital employed
- directors' salaries/owners' drawings

- cash-flow
- wage bill, and so forth.

While these financial measures are commendable, to some degree they miss the point. What really matters is far more than just the financials.

While I don't dispute the importance of finance - it is poor financial performance that will make you go bust - you need to recognise that:

> *"finance is simply a consequence of two other factors, marketing and operations..."*

SO WHAT?

To sort your *financial* performance you probably need to sort your *marketing* or *operations* performance.

WHAT DO WE MEAN BY *MARKETING* AND *OPERATIONS?*

Marketing is all about finding prospects and selling to them. There are as many measures of *marketing* as there are measures of *finance*.

Operations is all about producing the service or product. It is all about the 'doing'. There are as many measures of *operations* as there are of *finance*.

THOUGHT BUBBLE

Most agency people are too much in love with their agency. More specifically, they are too much in love with their product/service.

Most are preoccupied with the *making*. In other words, *operations*.

Great *operations* is of little value if you can't feed the machine via *marketing*!

SO, HOW GOOD IS YOUR AGENCY?

How would we measure your agency performance to date? What measures would we use to evaluate how good your agency is?

Score Your Agency, Now

Right now, score your agency. Take each of the three main headings in the table below and give your agency a score out of ten (where 0 is a very low score and 10 is a very high score).

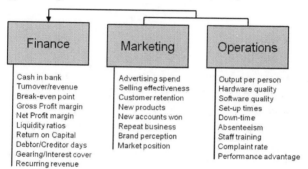

Agency Performance (FiMO)

Finance	Marketing	Operations
Cash in bank	Advertising spend	Output per person
Turnover/revenue	Selling effectiveness	Hardware quality
Break-even point	Customer retention	Software quality
Gross Profit margin	New products	Set-up times
Net Profit margin	New accounts won	Down-time
Liquidity ratios	Repeat business	Absenteeism
Return on Capital	Brand perception	Staff training
Debtor/Creditor days	Market position	Complaint rate
Gearing/Interest cover		Performance advantage
Recurring revenue		

Robert-Craven.com © 2015

How do the scores work?
- Scores of *2 or 3* suggest that there is something seriously wrong
- Scores of *4 or 5 or 6* suggest mediocrity
- Scores of *8 or 9* suggest that you are pretty good if not heading towards 'world class'.

ACTION

So, here goes... mark your scores out of ten. Remember that this scoring system is subjective; it should be your gut response. By definition, this process is a little ambiguous and that is because we are interested in the process, the discussion, about what the scores mean and how they can be improved. As soon as you enter a number, you (or your colleagues) can argue why the score given was either too high or too low.

For instance, if you give yourselves 7 for *Finance*, then ask,
- *Why haven't you given yourself 8 or 6?*
- *What would you need to do to improve the score?*
- *Is it 7 and improving, 7 and getting worse, or just stuck at 7?*
- *How can you justify your scores? Where is the evidence?*
- *Are you really sure that you are measuring appropriately?*

In fact, write down the scores in the book, right here, on the page.
- ***Finance*** - measuring performance and effectiveness: [eg cash/turnover/profit/sales]
- ***Marketing*** - measuring performance/effectiveness: [eg getting the right clients, your leads to client ratio...]
- ***Operations*** – doing the doing [eg how good you are at delivering your product or service].

LEARNING POINT

When scoring their own agency, most people score something like:

Finance	5
Marketing	3
Operations	8

– ie *financial* performance is OK, *marketing* is pretty poor and yet we feel that we are pretty good at the *operations*, the doing.

If you want to improve your *financial* score then improve your *marketing* performance (because most of us feel that we are pretty good at *operations*).

KEY POINT

A marketing expert will look for and see marketing issues as the key to a business situation; and an accountant will look for and see the financial issues. The *FiMO* framework gives us a much more balanced view of how the agency has performed.

So, you need to recognise that we have three interlocking and overlapping functions, both co-existing and interdependent. The image to be held in mind is that of a juggler – when all the balls move smoothly then there are no problems, but if one ball starts to misbehave then chaos ensues.

TWO MORALS HERE

First, you need to know your 'performance to date' (*'where are we now?'*) to establish your journey and direction.

Second, in order to improve your *financial* performance, it appears that you must first sort your *marketing* performance.

SPOILER ALERT

Actually you must first sort your finance model so that you are making a decent profit when you make a sale; only then should you increase your marketing activity.

LEARNING POINT

Most agencies score their *marketing* pretty low and their *operations* pretty high. If *finance* is an average of *marketing* and *operations* then if you improve your *marketing* then your *finance* should improve. It will improve more if you sort your *finance* model first.

WHAT CAN YOU DO RIGHT NOW?

1. Score your agency using the *FiMO* framework.
2. Identify and recognise your weaknesses.
3. Write up a list of three things you can do, starting tomorrow morning at 09:00hrs, to improve your scores.
4. Take action.

Where Do You Want To Be?

A large part of the strategy piece is debating and discussing where you want the agency to be (and why).

Planning from where you are today is almost impossible... so many immediate things that need to be dealt with... so many small things that just aren't quite right.

However, if you **start with the end in mind** then it is much easier to map out the journey and the steps on the way.

In the title of the chapter, the YOU refers not just to the agency but to you as the business owner-director.

ACTION - THE THREE BY THREE MATRIX

Ask yourself:

Where do I want *the agency* to be in three years' time?
So, where do I want *the agency* to be in one year's time?
So, what do I need to do now?

Where do I want *my professional life* to be in three years' time?

So, where do I want my *professional life* to be in one year's time?
So, what do I need to do now?

Where do I want *my private life* to be in three years' time?
So, where do I want *my private life* to be in one year's time?
So, what do I need to do now?

START WITH THE END IN MIND FOR THE BUSINESS

Clarity about direction and trajectory is crucial. At the same time, you do need to work through the exercise, if only to make your mistakes on paper. You should spend at least a day a year stepping back and looking at where you want to be in three years' time.

You can use the same categories as your *FiMO* scores to start the plan. If you currently measure turnover, cash, profit, staff numbers, client numbers, average client value, recurring income as % of total, Adword spend, then you can use the same categories for three years' time. As soon as you start writing down the new numbers you will start to check if and how the model fits together (or not).

This exercise should be done with the senior team or senior decision-makers.

The exercise covers the following:

1. Where are we now?

    (Use the *FiMO* exercise) See also the *RECoIL* framework in my book, *Kick-Start Your Business*.

2. Where are we going?

3. How are we going to get there?

THE CASCADE

To develop a working model of where you want to be requires creating a *"Cascade"* that helps you to clarify and define where you want to be. It is a fill-in-the-boxes exercise but really the value is in the thinking not just the writing of the words. It is a one-page exercise. Do not get caught up in the definitions of objectives, purpose, vision... everyone defines them differently. That's why I refer to them as Level 1 etc. It is the thinking that matters.

Fill in the following:

Level 0 – AKA *'Purpose'*

What is your purpose, your reason, for doing what you do? What is your 'Why?' Why do you exist?

Level 1 – AKA *'Vision'*

What is your 'Blue Skies' vision for the agency? What does success look like in, say, three years?

This is not about hard numbers but about what you want to be.

eg to be known as, to be in top three, to be recognised as...

Level 2 – AKA *'Mission'*

The numbers:

eg turnover, profit, staff, average client value, number of key clients...

Level 3 – AKA *'Strategy'*

How we are going to do it:

eg competing on price, competing on quality, best customer service, buying other agencies, hiring the best...

Level 4 – AKA *'Milestones'*

Steps on the way:

eg 20th employee, new premises, hiring a BusDev Director, hitting 25% Net Profit...

Level 5 – AKA *'Key Performance Indicators'* or KPIs

Key measures that matter (*"what gets measured gets done"*)

eg turnover, profit, cash, outstanding invoices, new clients, proposal conversion, complaints...

The exercise helps you clarify your thinking. Believe me. One page. One hour. Go for it.

THE WALLPAPER EXERCISE

The best way to map out the *"Where are we now? Where are we going? How are we going to get there?"* exercise is to plot your path on a long piece of wallpaper with the months written across the top from *"Today"* to *"Today +36 months"* where you can start to piece together the targets and the required resources as well as timings and order of work.

ACTION - DO THE WALLPAPER EXERCISE

If you haven't got a roll of wallpaper to hand then do a mini-wallpaper exercise using two pieces of A4 taped together. Plot current performance and 3-year goals, then fill in the steps on the way.

GOVERNMENT HEALTH WARNING

The creation of the wallpaper is the start of a bigger process, a process that will make it easier to run and lead the business. A process that will help you to understand, agree, gain buy-in and achieve your goals quicker and with less pain.

Imagining the vision for three years' time is more of an art than a science. Who really knows how things will change for customers, competitors, in the marketplace, in the industry or what changes will occur (political, economic, societal, technological, legislative, and environmental). The Three Year Goal is an aspiration, an articulation of the direction and rate of trajectory that you intend to follow. A way of making your mistakes on paper.

The reality is that having put together the big plan then you really need to focus on the next 90, 60, and 30 days. It is all very well planning a great plane trip but first you have to get off the runway!

A Dashboard For The Journey

It is one thing to run a *'Strategy Awayday'* to give you a grasp of *"Where are we now? Where are we going? How are we going to get there?"* However, making it happen is a very different kettle of fish.

One of the outputs from the wallpaper exercise is a more detailed business plan.

Before you shriek in horror, I am not talking about a heavyweight 250-page marathon. I am talking about a clear explanation of the who, what, where, why, when and how of the various aspects of your business. Strategy, Finance, Marketing Operations and People plans are the normal headings and the emphasis should be on **targets** and **how** you are going to achieve them.

On a monthly basis your senior management team (or board) needs to meet to track progress against the wallpaper. I would suggest a simple dashboard to tell you the basics. Referring back to the *FiMO* exercise I would opt for a maximum of four measures in each of four boxes as follows:

- Finance
- Marketing
- Operations

- Growth.

This dashboard is like the lights in an airplane cockpit measuring the critical and vital things:

> *'How high? How much fuel? How fast are we going? How far to go?'*

In the case of your business you measure the things (quantitative and qualitative) that will be indicators of how you are doing.

This exercise is worth its weight in gold. It will help you decide what is and what is not important. It will help you to focus on the real results and not the vanity figures that can so easily distract us.

ACTION - QUICK 'N' DIRTY

Select four measures for each of Finance, Marketing, Operations and Growth. Make sure that measuring these criteria will inform you of your performance.

In real time, this exercise should come <u>after</u> agreeing your Purpose, Vision, Mission, Strategy, Core Success Factors and Key Performance Indicators.

State Of The Nation

With a dashboard in place you are now ready to run a monthly meeting with the dashboard or scorecard at the centre.

The *State of the Nation* is a document that you produce monthly. You can then run your meeting around it. The result is that your board meetings are now focused on strategy and results rather than tactics or finance alone. Finance becomes the facilitator and not the policeman!

Everything needs to be described in four bullet points or less.

We are looking for clarity and focus and do not want to get bogged down with the minutiae of the detail. That is for another meeting.

This meeting is about how we are doing (against the wallpaper) and what we need to do more (or less) of.

SAMPLE STATE OF THE NATION AGENDA

Agenda: **Date:**

1. Actions Outstanding

2. Agenda Items To Discuss

3. Summary   (4 bullet points)

4. Dashboard Summary   (4 bullet points)

5. Dashboard

6. Financial Performance   (4 bullet points)

7. Marketing Performance   (4 bullet points)

8. Operations Performance   (4 bullet points)

9. Profit Centre #1 Performance   (4 bullet points)

10. Profit Centre #2 Performance   (4 bullet points)

11. Profit Centre #3 Performance   (4 bullet points)

12. Actions

Stand Out

AN EXAMPLE:

DIGITAL MARKETING EXHIBITION, LONDON

35 exhibition stalls stood side-by-side. Then there was one set back from the rest, in the corner.

I visited every stall. At each stall, I stood watching till a young twenty-something-year-old stepped forward and asked if they could help me.

My reply was always the same:
> *"Just looking to see what you do."*

The reply was identical within 5%. It always started with:
> *"We..."*
> *"We are... We do... We can.... We will..."*

It was all about them. Never about me, the customer. They just went into transmission mode. Virtually none of the 35 asked me:

who I was...

or

what my business was...

or

why I was interested in talking to a digital agency...

or
whether I already had one…
or
whether I was happy…
or
what I was looking for…

As I said, it was all about them.

I subsequently asked additional questions:
> *"Why should I buy from you when I can buy from the others?"*
> and/or
> *"What makes you different from the other stalls?"*

None could answer these questions head-on.

Some told me about their incredible high-profile client lists or their dubious celebrity relationships but none spoke to the questions. Most mentioned good value-for-money and high ROI or being customer-focused but none gave examples, proof or evidence to support the claims. It was marketing noise. All speeches they had learnt in the vain hope that it would impress.

Also, none talked about specific results or fees.
Fail. Fail. Fail.

Incredibly disappointing.

WHAT DID I, A POTENTIAL CLIENT, WANT TO KNOW?

The simple question behind my enquiries was:

> *"What can you do for me...? And, do give me some numbers (results and costs) to help me make a decision whether I should buy from you."*

Fail. Fail. Fail.

THE MIDDLE-AGED BLOKE IN THE CORNER

They all failed. Apart from the one in the corner, headed up by a fifty-something-year-old bloke looking less cool than the other agencies. His approach was entirely different.

His opening question to me was:

> *"Hi, tell me about your business and why you might be talking to a digital agency?"*

He said little and listened a lot as I described my current digital strategy and results to date. He asked great questions that made me think and made me realise he knew his stuff.

When I finally asked:

> *"Why should I buy from you... what makes you different...?"*

his answer was simple:

> *"We are the only agency here that, one, works almost exclusively with professional service firms like yours and, two, charges by results only. No results, no fee. We have to really understand your objectives if we want to get paid."*

Game, set and match to the fifty-year-old in the corner.

QUESTION
Do you stand out from the crowd?

MARKETING

In other words,

HOW CAN YOU GET MORE OF THE PEOPLE YOU WANT... TO BUY YOUR STUFF?

In some senses, I shouldn't need to be writing about marketing in a book aimed at digital agencies.

This should be your bread and butter.

After all, what you do for your clients is help them to get more and better clients. So, the very same skillset that you apply to a client's business needs to be applied to your own.

At its simplest the principles I will cover will show you how to:

- deliver more successful campaigns for your clients
- run a more effective agency of your own.

And the principles are not rocket science but just very powerful. They focus on basic buyer psychology and presenting yourself in a way that builds on the three cornerstones of:

- Relevance
- Engagement
- Reputation.

The key questions that you need to be able to answer for your own agency (and that you need to ask to help clients) are:

1. What is your **Marketing Strategy?**
2. Which **segments** of the market are you focusing on?
3. How are you **differentiated** from the rest?

4. What is your **USP?**
5. What is your **Quantifiable Customer Value Proposition?**
6. What is your **Elevator Pitch** (say 3, for different occasions)?
7. What are the **brand message, voice and personality?**
8. What is your **sales process?**

Marketing/Sales: S&M or M&S

There is plenty of debate about the thin line between *Marketing* and *Sales* and about how they do or do not work together and how they should never be left alone in a room without a minder!

Yes, marketing is theoretically about finding and wooing clients, and yes, sales is theoretically about making the sale, and yes, they do squabble and have turf wars but really they should and must be pulling in the same direction.

AGENCIES ARE RARELY THE BEST MARKETERS

Ironically, most digital agencies are not so great at S&M or M&S themselves. They may understand the nuts and bolts of how to assemble a campaign, but many fail to create and deliver a successful programme for themselves. If they did, then they would all be inundated with exactly the work they really want to be doing.

For me, marketing is all about results. In fact my colleague Martin says that we should never use the word marketing but call it *'revenue generation'*. If it doesn't generate revenue then why are we doing it?

Earlier on we said marketing is about:

> *why and how...we get which people...to buy what from us...*

At its heart, it is not about likes, clicks, followers or conversion rate but about making sales, and profitable sales at that.

Marketing Hierarchy

In the same way that there is a hierarchy for working through the model (strategy, marketing, teams, people, operations, processes) so there is a hierarchy for ordering your marketing.

To get your marketing house in order I suggest you figure out the following and in the following order:

- Marketing Strategy/Strategic Marketing Plan
- Market Segmentation and Differentiation
- USP
- Value Proposition
- Elevator Pitch (say 3, for different occasions)
- Marketing Channels
- Sales Process
- Proposal Templates.

Marketing Strategy

Right through the marketing chapters I will keep asking the same two questions:

> *"Why should people bother to buy from you when they can buy from the competition?*
>
> and
>
> *"What makes you different from the rest?"*

Put another way, your marketing strategy needs to address:

> *why and how... we get which people... to buy what from us*

While this is not the place to go into the full level of detail required, I do think that we should mention that you need to have a proper understanding of:

- the target customer's wants, needs and hurts
- the competitive landscape.

We are talking about:

- segmenting the market(s)
- differentiating your offer(s).

My book, *Bright Marketing,* covers this in a lot more detail. Suffice to say, your marketing is a combination of science (doing the numbers and the research) and art (the creative piece.)

Strategic Marketing Plan

A typical Strategic Marketing Plan might include the following headings:

1. Executive Summary
2. The Purpose Statement
3. Financial Summary
4. Market Overview - including relevant segments and their needs
5. SWOT Analyses (segments)
6. Portfolio Summary
7. Assumptions
8. Objectives and Strategies
9. Budget

For more on strategic marketing plans, segmentation and differentiation, read Prof Malcolm McDonald on the subject.

Segment Your Marketplace

I hear you ask,
> *"Why segment my client marketplace?"*

And the answer is because:
1. All segments are not equal.
2. Each segment requires a different approach.
3. You need to prioritise segments according to opportunity, gaps and your capability.
4. Segments love a tailored approach.

In a nutshell, you need to ask the following so that you can refine and design your offering to match the individual segment requirements:

- **What is and will be bought and why?**
    Benefits, usage, prices, channels, how and when bought
- **Who buys and why?**
    Role, personality, attitude, goals
- **Are the market segments big enough?**
    Are they reachable? Are they different?

ACTION

Use the segmentation table below as a template to define and articulate the differences between the segments that you score. This is a bit of a hit-or-miss exercise as you play with the different segment definitions. (Part science, part art!)

SIMPLE SEGMENTATION TABLE

Segment Name:	1	2	3	4

Who? Demographic
        Geographic
        Psychographic				

What product and benefits?				
Where/Which channel?				
When? How often?				
How? Payment type?				
Why? Benefits sought? Advantage sought?				
Price?				

Differentiation

You can differentiate yourself by identifying your unique characteristics and highlighting them.

The way you position and differentiate yourself in the context of:
1. The competition, and
2. The clients' preferred buying patterns

will contribute to your success.

One more time:
> *"Why should people bother to buy from you when they can buy from the competition?"*
> and
> *"What makes you different from the rest?"*

Unique Selling Proposition

I do not wish to get drawn into the subtleties of what is and what is not a USP. Call it what you will, you need to be able to articulate what makes you different from the rest.

WHY IS THIS IMPORTANT?

1. In order to articulate your customer value proposition and your elevator pitch, **you need to know and understand what it is that makes you special** (in the eyes of the client). Your brand, web, or PR agency will also need to know this.
2. The second question that people often ask after *"What is your business?"* is ***"What is your USP?"***

It seems dumb not to be able to answer a question you know you are going to be asked.

The USP was first proposed as a theory to explain a pattern in successful advertising campaigns of the early 1940s. Nowadays, the USP applies to answer the questions:

> *"What makes you special? What makes you different?"*

Saying anything that resembles *"We are the same as the competition"* is not clever or helpful.

Your Value Proposition

Simply put, a value proposition is:

> *"the promise of value to be delivered and the belief from the customer point of view that value will be experienced."*

However, what I am really talking about is a **quantifiable customer value proposition**:

> *"the promise of quantified value to be delivered and the belief from the customer point of view that quantified value will be experienced."*

Very few businesses actually use a Value Proposition to describe what they do, never mind a quantifiable one. They should. Clients just love to be given a compelling reason to buy that is not all smoke and mirrors.

THE PROOF

Looking at 4,000 campaigns, Doug Hall, business author, discovered that sales success dramatically improved when sales presentations combine the following three characteristics:

- the **overt business benefit** that you offer
- the **real reason that people should believe** you can deliver

- the **dramatic difference** that separates you from the crowd.

This makes sense.

Your ability to describe what it is that you do directly impacts on your ability to win work. It is worth spending time honing and crafting a value proposition so that you can answer those tough questions like:

> *"why should we buy from you?"* and *"what exactly can you do for us?"*

BE CLEAR

Make the benefits explicit, make the price/cost/investment explicit, and make the target customer explicit.

Be clear about how this value proposition is superior for the people in front of you in terms of added value, cost reduction, cost avoidance and/or feelgood factors.

EXAMPLE 1:

> *XYZ's £3,500 per month 3-star package includes all aspects of creating and delivering the e-commerce and web presence for mid-tier accountants. We guarantee qualified leads will increase (by 15%) and this will lead to 8 new clients* pm. Typically,*

increased revenues of £480,000 pa (annualised). We are the only agency in this market that makes such a guarantee.

* typically at £5k pa

EXAMPLE 2

ABC is your Adword partner. For £10,575 pa, we put you on page one of Google and deliver 100 leads per month. The value to your practice in terms of direct fees alone will be in excess of £40,000 pa. We are the only agency working with dentists and doctors that promises and delivers such an offer.

While these don't answer every question perfectly you have to admire them.

I would argue that you need to refine your **quantifiable customer value proposition** until you can articulate it in an instantly credible manner.

Most value propositions answer the question,
"Why should our firm purchase your offering?"

Some answer the question,
"Why should our firm purchase your offering instead of your competition's?"

And, the best answer the question,

> *"What is most worthwhile for us to keep in mind about your offering?"*

GOOD NEWS, BAD NEWS

Prof Malcolm McDonald believes that only 4% of companies/suppliers have a quantifiable customer value proposition. He is probably right. Bad news for the customers of 96% of suppliers, good news for 4% of companies that have one.

ACTION

Create your own quantifiable customer value proposition.

Elevator Pitch (x3)

Once you have crafted your quantifiable customer value proposition you can create your elevator pitch.

"What's the difference?" I hear you ask.

While the customer value proposition is the headline statement that informs so much of your marketing communications, the elevator pitch answers the informal question we so often get asked at networking meetings etc - *"So, what do you do?"* It is a friendly, colloquial way of communicating you proposition.

So here's a template:

We work with…

> Be specific – define by type of business, age of business, size of business, type of person, etc.

Who have a problem with…

> Focus on what 'pain' they are in – what are they looking for a solution to; focus on the negative pain (who *can't get enough* customers) rather than the positive (who *want more* customers) as it's more powerful that way.

What we do is...

What do you do that resolves the problem?
eg we act as your digital department.

So that...

This should be a simple explanation of the 'thing'
that the customer gets or can do now,
eg *you have a more search engine friendly website.*

Which means...

List the benefits,
eg *you get more customers or you convert more
visitors into customers.*

AN EXAMPLE

We work with...

Major, full service marketing agencies

Who have a problem with...

*Maintaining a digital department at the cutting edge
(of latest search engine optimisation and
management techniques)*

What we do is...

*Act as an outsourced white label department that
appears to be part of the main team*

So that...

> *The big marketing company can concentrate on developing the customer strategy and focus on core account management knowing that the digital piece will be executed seamlessly*

Which means...

> *The marketing agency client gets the top level focus as well as beautiful execution of the digital strategy. The end client gets what they want and the marketing agency offers a profitable service without the hassle of running its own department.*

ANOTHER EXAMPLE

We work with...

> *Small and medium-sized businesses in the North*

Who have a problem with...

> *Being sold digital turkeys... promises of unbounded web traffic and qualified leads that never materialise*

What we do is...

> *Design and create a digital strategy that delivers on the marketing strategy. Like clockwork. We are your outsourced digital partner rewarded for performance not time*

So that…

> *You don't need to worry about the digital piece. It's sorted. It delivers as agreed (or your money back)*

Which means…

> *You get all the benefits of having your own digital department without the hassle. More importantly, you can concentrate on what you are good at, wooing and closing sales that have been delivered on a silver plate.*

ACTION

Create at least three elevator pitches appropriate for different target customers, products or markets.

Marketing Channels

I am going to go light on this one! It deserves a book in its own right.

Once you have established who your target customer is and how and why and when they buy, then you can select the most appropriate channels to reach them.

Please recognise that the choice of channels becomes 'obvious' only when you have done the preceding marketing work. This applies to you and your business as well as to your clients' businesses. There are no obvious solutions as to the best channels. No one-size-fits-all solution.

EXAMPLE 1

For my business, 95% comes from word-of-mouth recommendations and referrals so that is what I nurture.

EXAMPLE 2

My friend Jim's agency gets half of its new work from word-of-mouth, the other half as a result of a book he wrote.

EXAMPLE 3

Another agency uses a garish, loud and provocative 16 pillars approach and tries to access clients through every one with an incredibly consistent message and argues that all channels deliver a healthy ROI. She uses:

> *"email campaigns, Adword campaigns, exhibitions, leaflet drops, letters, newsletters, telesales, free books, blogs, seminars, workshops, affiliate programmes, educational programmes, TV and radio advertising, landing pages"...*

as well as SEO and SEM.

EXAMPLE 4

Another agency I work with gets nearly half of its work from exhibiting at shows (the other half is from word-of-mouth!)

So, the best or most optimum marketing channel(s) will depend on your target client, your USP and your customer value proposition. However, the common theme here is that of word-of-mouth.

You must nurture the power of creating a great reputation.

Sales Process

An understanding of the 'sales hopper', 'sales funnel' or 'sales pipeline' is required.

In a nutshell, most of your clients go through a process to go from being a stranger (or potential prospect) to becoming a client (my old *'strangers, friends and lovers'* routine).

THE SALES PIPELINE STAGES

Here's a typical list of the stages that the potential client might pass through:

1. Prospect? Do they have a need?
2. We communicate.
3. They see us, they're interested.
4. A Try Before You Buy – they like it.
5. They say they want to buy.
6. Letter of intent.
7. Purchase order/contract.
8. Money in the bank.

As the prospect moves from stage to stage (down the hopper, or along the sales pipeline or funnel, depending on your preferred analogy) so the likelihood of success increases –

you could allocate probabilities at each stage if you wish. (I suggest you do!)

The point behind this is as follows:

- Understand the steps that people go through to become clients
- Understand how many potential clients are at each stage
- Calculate the probability of future income streams
    - multiply expected income times the probability of success to get to know the likelihood of someone becoming a paying client
- It gets you thinking about how you can move the potential clients to the next stage
- It gets you thinking about how you can qualify people:
    - Are you talking to the right person?
    - Do they have spending power?
    - Do they want to buy right now?
    - Are they talking to anyone else?
    - Have they bought this type of service before?

This helps you to establish whether you are talking to a time-waster/tyre-kicker or someone who you would really like as a client.

AND IN PRACTICE

Below we have reproduced a sample hopper system, as used by Jane Sampson's agency.

"We have the hopper up on the wall so we can see who we are chasing and how far we've got with them. It stops us from letting leads fall through our fingers and keeps us on track. We've combined this with a Lead Interrogator which makes us ask ourselves questions like:

- *Are we talking to the right person?*
- *Is the hurt big enough?*
- *Will we be able to exceed their expectations?*

We update it every Monday morning - this works for us."

Company	Our A/C Manager	Lead	Conversation	Proposal	Client	Follow-up Date
Co 1	JJ	Yes				18 Sept
Co 2	TG	Yes				10 Sept
Co 3	JS	Yes	Yes			23 Sept
Co 4	JS	Yes	Yes	Yes		23 Sept
Co 5	TG	Yes	Yes	Yes	Yes	1 Oct
Co 6	JS	Yes	Yes	Yes	Yes	10 Oct

ACTION POINTS

Describe your ideal client.

- How would they approach you?
- How would they present their problem/hurt to you?
- What stages would they go through from being a stranger to becoming a client?
- Is there any way that you can encourage them to move through the hopper faster?
- Do you lose any of them on the way, and if so, why?
- What questions would you have to ask to establish whether it was worth your while to pursue them as a potential client?

SYSTEMS ARE EVERYTHING

The more that you are able to systemise your offering and your approach to business, the more you are able to predict the outcome of your activities.

Creating systems involves being clear about what you wish to achieve. You need to test all your activities to find the most effective methods – it is a continual process where you constantly seek out smarter and cleverer ways of getting what you want.

And, of course, systems are repeatable. And scaleable.

The Sales Funnel Is Dead

Many, myself included, feel that the sales funnel is now dead. Clients don't behave as the hopper suggests; maybe they never did.

Clients just do not act as the model says they should: they skip steps or sometimes they stall in certain places.

The process is less of a funnel and more of an interconnected set of events (see the ZMOT ideas from Google).

However, I still rate the hopper as a way of managing and tracking leads. Warts and all.

The pdf, "The Sales Funnel is Dead", can be seen at http://robert-craven.com/the-sales-funnel-is-dead-long-live-the-king/

Proposal Template

Please note that most clients are not that interested in how you are going to do what you promise to achieve (whether it is one or two people at one or two hours a day is really not the issue).

The issue is far more around what I, the client, get for my money that will help me.

> *"People do not buy what you do. They buy what you do... does for them."*

And most clients of digital agencies want more profit from more sales from more leads and better conversions.

More importantly, the proposal is not about you; it is all about the client.

To avoid endlessly re-inventing the wheel it makes sense to create a series of proposal templates.

95% of people have attended a dreadful cookie cutter workshop on proposal writing and as result most proposals follow a similar format starting with:

> *"We were formed in 1999... We have 10 years' experience... We... We... blah blah."*

It is all about the agency.

As a client, I do not really care. What I, as the client, care about is:

> *"How well do you understand my business, my problems and my issues? And how are you going to solve them? More importantly, how much is it going to cost and what will I get for my money in terms of results for my business?"*

However, before you even put pen to paper may I suggest that you ask the client how they want the proposal presented to them. This way you guarantee to give them what they want and save wasting everyone's time.

Our experience in asking the question is that there are a variety of replies and you are able to demonstrate your client focus by responding as requested.

Clients will say a number of different things. Here are a selection:

- *"Just send me a one-page outline proposal then we can work from there."*
- *"Make sure you show me exactly what services are included in the price."*
- *"Include three cases studies and I want the names of three people I can phone as references."*
- *"My FD needs to see everything including your insurance cover, Health and Safety, Equality and Quality Procedures and Policies."*

- *"Our procurement division will send you the standard supplier template that is required to be filled in by all suppliers."*

All these conversations happened.

SAMPLE TEMPLATE

1. Executive Summary
     Snappy title... the issue... the solution... the benefits... the return on investment... the fee... snappy close.
2. Client Goals & Objectives.
3. Client Issues.
4. Our Solution.
5. Recommended Services (and why).
6. Fee Schedule, Guarantees.
7. Why Choose Us (include Testimonials, Case Studies URLs).
8. Schedule of Work.
9. Next Steps.
10. Terms and Conditions.

Read the proposal as if you are a client.

Ask *"So what?"* or *"So what does that mean to me?"* or *"Why should I care?"* to every statement in the proposal. If in doubt in the writing stage, add the phrase *"which means that..."* to emphasise the benefit to the client.

Don't just write:

> *"All our people have this year's Google Partner training on Adwords."*

Write:

> *"All our people have this year's Google Partner training on Adwords **which means that** you have access to the latest, most up-to-date facts about maximising Adword spend to attract the best most profitable clients for your business."*

Remember that the covering email/letter is as important as the proposal itself and reflects the quality and degree of care that you apply to each and every process. So, please make sure that you cover the key points succinctly. You will be measured on your ability to clearly and simply articulate what it is that you are going to do.

Pause For Thought

To summarise what has been said.

Great agencies are obsessed with:

1. **Strategy**
   Where are we going and how are we going to get there?
2. **Marketing**
   Why... which people should buy what from us.

If you can sort this out then the rest becomes relatively straightforward.

.

MONEY

In other words,

PROFIT and CASH

We Need To Talk About Prices

The *FiMO* model tells us that in order to sort our finances we need to sort out our marketing. (For most agencies, *Operations* are pretty good so to improve *Financial* performance you need to improve *Marketing* performance).

But, and this is a big but... Before you can sort out your financial performance you have to sort out your financial model. So how do you do it?

PUT PRICES UP? PUT PRICES DOWN?

People always ask about whether to put up prices or reduce them. Please, please, think very carefully before you consider putting prices down. Let me explain my thinking.

THE ROAD TO BANKRUPTCY

The road to bankruptcy is paved with people who tried to buy customers or market share by cutting prices.

In my humble opinion...

Always try to avoid a price war, as it is unlikely that you will be the winner. There is always a bigger player who has bigger marketing power, bigger buying power and deeper pockets. You will end up reducing your margins... Some competitors/people may go out of business... (They euphemistically describe this as a 'shakeout' in the industry!) And you'll get less profit per sale than you got before.

The other option is to raise prices.

A MYTH

"You must lower prices to keep or get the business."
Wrong!

THE STAGGERING TRUTH

"The average proportion of consumers across all categories who were motivated by price was around 10 per cent and even if this increased during a downturn, the proportion would remain small."
[Advertising in a Downturn, IPA]

"Cutting prices is usually insanity if the competition can go as low as you can."
[Prof M Porter, Harvard Bus Schl]

PRICE CHANGES IN A NUTSHELL

Lowering prices probably attracts the wrong clients and eats into your profitability. Raising prices means you lose the pond life and become more profitable. I know which one I prefer.

WHAT HAPPENS WHEN YOU RAISE PRICES?

Inevitably you will lose some customers when you put up prices.

However, the clients you normally lose are those that are *'buying on price'* – to me these are normally what I would describe as 'pond life', clients you would be happy to see the back of... They buy on price, pay late and always want more. You don't need these types of clients.

And the irony is... that your most profitable clients often don't notice the change in prices because they aren't buying on price alone; they are buying on quality or value-added.

Profit Improvement Checklist

Below is a list of profitability tactics (in descending order of impact on profit health):

1. Raise the selling price.
2. Lower the cost of sales.
3. Focus on the profitable lines and drop the under-performers.
4. Increase volume.
5. Lower overheads.

TACTICS ONE AND TWO: RAISE THE SELLING PRICE: LOWER THE COST OF SALES

The first two items, selling price and cost of sales, are all about Gross Profit margin. Beware of 'GP Drift'. So often we forget to look at Gross Profit. Assumptions are made about pricing and job costing; we use our usual suppliers and forget to renegotiate prices and terms of trade. Look for any fat you may have allowed to creep in and eliminate it, now.

You can earn higher prices by specialising and by adding more value to the customer (doing it better).

Or you can use marketing to get better contracts (do it better or do it nicer).

Likewise you can improve your business efficiency (do it faster or do it cheaper). You must develop systems to speed up how you deliver value to the customer.

TACTIC ONE: RAISING THE SELLING PRICE

The tables below enable you to calculate the change in sales volume that can be accommodated to compensate for a change in price and yet still maintain your Gross Profit margin. Conversely, you could use these charts to estimate the impact of changes in Gross Margin percentages.

Table to show the decrease in sales volume that can be accommodated to compensate for an increase in price and yet still maintain your Gross Profit margin.

% price increase	Existing percentage gross margin								
	5	10	15	20	25	30	35	40	50
⇩	Percentage unit/volume decrease to generate same gross margin								
2.0	29	17	12	9	7	6	5	5	4
3.0	37	23	17	13	11	9	8	7	6
4.0	44	29	21	17	14	12	10	9	7
5.0	50	33	25	20	17	14	12	11	9
7.5	60	43	33	27	23	20	18	16	13
10.0	67	50	40	33	29	25	22	20	17
15.0	75	60	50	43	37	33	30	27	23

Table to show the increase in sales volume that needs to be accommodated to compensate for a decrease in price and yet still maintain your Gross Profit margin.

% price reduction ⇩	Existing percentage gross margin								
	5	10	15	20	25	30	35	40	50
	Percentage unit/volume increase to generate same gross margin								
2.0	67	25	15	11	9	7	6	5	4
3.0	150	43	25	18	14	11	9	8	6
4.0	400	67	36	25	19	15	13	11	9
5.0		100	50	33	25	20	17	14	11
7.5		300	100	60	43	33	27	23	18
10.0			200	100	67	50	40	33	25
15.0				300	150	100	75	60	43

CASE STUDY EXAMPLE

RHT, an agency, was turning over £450,000 with a gross margin of 40% (after all direct costs). Judi, the owner, was considering the impact of price changes.

The tables clearly indicated the following:

- A price increase of 4% would mean that she would generate the same gross margin (£s) even if sales volumes fell by 9%

- A price increase of 5% would mean that she would generate the same gross margin (£s) even if sales volumes fell by 11%
- A price increase of 10% would mean that she would generate the same gross margin (£s) even if sales volumes fell by 20%.

Judi:

> *"I decided to put prices up by 10%. The risk paid off. Volumes did drop but only by a small amount, later calculated to be about 5%. The net effect was beneficial to all – less activity, less output, greater profits."*

TACTIC ONE: RAISE THE SELLING PRICES – THE EVIDENCE

In one year, I asked the following question to over 6,000 business owners,

> *"Have you put up your prices in the last three months?"*

Roughly 7.5% said,

> *"Yes!"*

I then asked a simple question of the 450 owners who had put up their prices,

> *"Did any of you lose money as a result of putting up your prices?"*

The answer was consistently,

"No!"

followed by one of these statements:

> *"We simply lost the bad customers - hurray!"*
> *"Sales rose because we were able to focus our efforts on the cream of our database."*
> *"We freed up so much time we had been wasting that we could start doing the profitable stuff."*
> *"If anything sales rose at every level!"*

TACTIC TWO: LOWER THE COST OF SALES

You can increase your Gross Profit margin by either putting up prices (see Tactic One above), or cutting direct costs.

To be blunt, I call lowering the cost of sales:

> *"Screwing your suppliers' feet to the ground on price."*

Have you been to every one of your suppliers and asked if they can offer you a better deal or package?

It is amazing how they can suddenly offer you a discount rather than lose your business. But you have to ask for it!

The trick is to ask the *'best price'* question and then say nothing till they answer you. It might feel like an eternity but very few people want to lose your business.

My favourite lines are:

> *"Is that the best price you can do?"*
>
> *"I don't want to move to a different supplier so is there something you can do on the price?"*

Ask the question then keep your mouth shut till they answer.

TACTIC THREE: FOCUS ON THE PROFITABLE LINES AND DROP THE UNDER-PERFORMERS

Once the GP drift has been sorted out, then attention can be turned to profitables:

- Which products/lines generate the real profit?
- And what activities generate little or no profit?

ACTION POINT

Focus on doing more with the highly profitable.

Deal with the under-performers – try and educate and if not, sack the under-performing:

- suppliers
- products and services
- customers
- staff.

Try and re-educate or sack them!

When looking at the profitables, look for **the 80/20 Rule** – 80% of outputs (profit) will be generated by 20% of inputs (customers, products, suppliers, staff, effort).

The 80/20 Rule - the principle of the vital few and the trivial many - says that most of our effort is a waste of time (the trivial many) so deal with the trivial many and don't accept the excuses such as *'non-profitable work is required to cover overheads'* or other such nonsense.

TACTIC FOUR: INCREASE VOLUME

Only when you have sorted out your GP drift and your under-performers can you look at increasing volume. To do so earlier would put you in a position of becoming an even busier fool than you were becoming in any case.

TACTIC FIVE: REDUCE THE OVERHEADS

When the first four steps have been followed you can then consider reducing overheads. To do so earlier sends all the wrong messages to your workforce – they do not appreciate downgrading their company cars and the damage to morale is immeasurable!

By lowering your overheads, you are improving efficiency again. Reducing support costs and resources and improving efficiency must be undertaken with care – otherwise any anticipated benefits may be outweighed by the proverbial 'false economies' and consequential backlash.

Profit Improvement Hacks

Here's an example of a quick 'n' dirty plan adopted by a recent client (an agency employing 16 people) – this activity turned the business around.

It is a series of small changes which, when combined, has a massive impact. No one activity on its own would have a great impact but when put together you can see that there is a huge benefit to the business.

Here's the first list:
1. Increase prices by 3%
2. Decrease direct costs by 3%
3. Increase number of leads by 3%
4. Increase quality of sales conversations by 3%
5. Increase quality of proposals by 3%
6. Increase quality of closes/asking for the business by 3%
7. Increase number of purchases by each customer by 3%
8. Decrease overheads by 3%.

They used my special calculator/excel spreadsheet and saw that the impact of these calculations was massive. I do not exaggerate.

For instance, the basic changes suggested above take a £500,000 a year business from £50,000 net profit to £121,900, an increase of over 100%! And that's before you adjust the figures for sacking under-performers or for the impact of sorting the cash-flow. (To be honest, these additional changes had not been put into the worksheets as they make the spreadsheet too complex – it would be easy for you to design a spreadsheet that reflects your specific business.)

And of course you would also want to do the following (which we have not included in the calculators):

9. Sort under-performing clients, products, suppliers, staff (sack 5%?)
10. Pull in cash 10 days faster.
11. Spend cash 10 days slower.

As I said, small changes but massive impact.

THOUGHT BUBBLE

What are you going to do to improve the profitability and cash-flow of your business?

We Need To Talk About Cash

Agencies normally go bust because they run out of cash. I can assure you that it is impossible to trade without cash: cash to grow, cash to invest, cash to pay, cash to take your business to the next level.

CASH-FLOW STATEMENTS

You must understand the cash-flow and working capital implication of your plans. Look at last year's cash-flow statement. If you don't know what I am talking about then find out about them now!

CASH-FLOW FORECASTS

Do not work on creating a 'realistic' cash-flow forecast. Work on a pessimistic one. Things are never/rarely as good as expected – cash haemorrhages from most agencies most of the time; at some point cash-flow, new leads and sales slow down. This will drive many a profitable business into the bankruptcy courts.

Run a 13-week cash-flow forecast and update it weekly. Why would you not?

BREAK-EVEN POINT (BEP)

To be clear, you must know the break-even point of each product line. If you don't know what I am talking about, then to quote the old board game,

'Do not pass GO, do not collect £200'.

Please find out about BEP now!

EXAMPLE IN PRACTICE

Business Systems UK's Stephen Thurston on Finance:

"Money drives or strangles a business. You have to understand how to read your own profit and loss account, why it is so important to have access to financial figures, and why it is so important to budget. For most people, those are not their prime considerations."

TEAMS, PEOPLE, OPERATIONS

In other words,

WHY CAN'T YOU GET ON BETTER AND MAKE AN EVEN BETTER PRODUCT?

Beyond The Tip Of The Iceberg

So, what we have discussed is the basics of setting up the business for growth and now it is time to get back to where we started which is the mindset of the growing agency owner-director.

As well as creating the intention and direction for growth you need to set up the right systems, processes and controls that will enable your people to deliver on the plan.

In such a short book we cannot cover every aspect but we do recognise that a plan is nothing without the actions and activities taking place.

To that end I would like to mention the dull, boring stuff.

In Praise Of Dull, Boring Stuff

Rarely am I asked,

> *"Speak to us about the dull, boring stuff we know we ought to be better at in our business: structure, operational efficiency, systems, processes, time management and relationships..."*

Of course, the irony is that it is the so-called dull, boring stuff that makes an agency above average, in the long run.

THE DIFFERENCE THAT MAKES THE DIFFERENCE

The great agencies do great work but they are also great at figuring out a **winning strategy** and **compelling marketing** as well as getting their **teams** to do all the nitty gritty.

Running an agency is a little like Formula 1:

> *"F1 cars are the same. The difference is the driver"*

SO, WHAT IS THIS DULL, BORING STUFF?

The four areas are:

1. Structure.
2. Time Management.
3. Operational Efficiency.
4. Relationships.

They are all interlinked and I will address them in this order.

Structure

Your structure needs to be appropriate to your size and scale of operations. As the business grows, your shape constantly morphs as you try to respond to outside pressures.

Clearly you need account managers, analysts, coders and so on to do the work, the Operations team. Also, you need an Administration and Finance function. But they would all be redundant if your Marketing and Sales function wasn't bringing in the clients.

In an ideal world the three functions interface and inter-relate. Often that is not the case.

Above the three functions you need a board or senior management team, the brain of the business. While the functions work **in** the business on a day-to-day basis, the board should be working **on** the business.

You need to create a mechanism that meets, ideally monthly, to look at the big picture, to monitor and evaluate progress on your wallpaper. (See State of the Nation, page 36).

At different sizes, your requirements will be different.

It is at key inflection points that the current/old structure will be stretched to its limits.

Think of the business lifecycle as a series of stages – a little like human stages of: baby, toddler, child, adolescent, adult.

For a business the stages are:
1. Growth through **Creativity**
2. Growth through **Direction**
3. Growth through **Delegation**
4. Growth through **Coordination**
5. Growth through **Collaboration**

Each stage of growth is characterised by a different impetus to grow and threatened by a different crisis. As one passes from one stage to another, it is critical for the owner to know when to relinquish control and delegate to others.

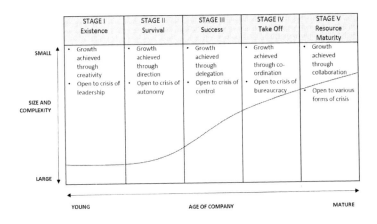

As the agency grows there is a clear trade-off between the owner's ability to execute and his/her ability to delegate. Some people can cross the chasm to the other side, from working IN to working ON the business. Others cannot.

	STAGE I Existence	STAGE II Survival	STAGE III Success	STAGE IV Take Off	STAGE V Resource Maturity
CRITICAL TO SUCCESS	Owner's ability to execute				
SIZE AND COMPLEXITY					
RELEVANT OR NATURAL BY-PRODUCT	Owner's ability to delegate				

Time Management

We've all been on time management courses that haven't worked.

Meanwhile, the great creatives and account directors manage their time better than others. At its simplest, this links into our earlier conversation about strategy.

Effective managers exhibit certain key traits that can be summed up as follows:

1. Be proactive.
2. *"Start with the end in mind"*.
3. Prioritise (*"first things first"*).
4. Think Win-Win (or no deal).
5. Communicate (*"seek first to understand"*).
6. Co-operate (1+1=3!!).
7. Stay fit (*"sharpen the saw"*).

   [Covey: 7 Habits of Effective People]

In other words, you need to take ownership and control. If you know what you are trying to achieve (strategy) then the prioritisation (management) becomes obvious. Given that you can sort these two issues then it becomes all about people and relationships – getting all of them aligned and firing on all cylinders. Easier said than done.

At its essence, my view of time management is that we need to be clear about the difference between:

- what is **important** (planning, organisation, structure), and
- what is **urgent** (what needs to be done now).

The more and the better we plan, the less urgent issues need to be attended to.

Prioritising and listing is part of the skillset required. Some are better than others at this but apps such as *Evernote* and *Toodledo* can help.

Operational Efficiency

Being technicians, digital people often try to create the best, most perfect solution rather than what is required. It is a fine art to tread the thin line between what is required by the client and what is possible.

Operational efficiency is useless if the client is not happy and we need to remember that our agencies are client-facing – after all they pay the bills.

So here's a question:

WHAT DO YOU WANT A CUSTOMER TO SAY AS A RESULT OF AN INTERACTION?

Well, all the customer experience books used to say that it was:

> *"Wow, they really went out of their way to delight me!"*

However, nowadays it is more likely to be:

> *"Wow, they really went out of their way to make it so much easier to solve my problem!"*

The reality is that low effort service (making it easy to buy and do business with you) equals high customer loyalty. Especially in the online world we now live in.

Relationships

The relationships piece presents itself in two directions:
- internally – with your team
- externally – with clients, partners and suppliers.

I got a very hostile reception when a blog of mine said:
> *"All great businesses are obsessed with:*
> - *Strategy*
> - *Marketing and*
> - *Teams (and people are a nightmare)".*

I was summoned to explain what I meant when I said ***"and people are a nightmare"***.

I wrote it because it is true.

We can design and manage strategy and marketing and operations and we can monitor and evaluate the effectiveness of such programmes and activities with the usual KPIs (Key Performance Indicators). However, the delivery is dependent on your people doing their part and that is where the nightmare comes in.

Often people who run digital agencies struggle with relationships. You start running a digital agency because you are great at doing all the digital, at-the-keyboard work. All task-driven and dealing with algorithms and the whole digital piece.

MANAGING PEOPLE IS TOUGH

However, I have to say that the great agencies get the people piece sorted as well. And that is a challenge in terms of recruiting, training, retaining, rewarding and managing your people, their expectations and their ability to deliver. Get it right and you are running a powerhouse. Get it wrong and it is like a living nightmare!

Similarly, great external relationships mean that you limit fighting and squabbling and you can run joint ventures and partnership arrangements where everyone can benefit. I do not under-estimate the skills of people who are good at relationships.

THE CHALLENGE

So, that is the challenge. Run a great agency that delivers. And do it by gathering together the power and force of the people inside and outside the business to help you achieve your goals.

Digital Agency Manifesto

MORE THAN A WHITE PAPER... ALMOST AN ASPIRATIONAL DOCTRINE – TO LEAD AGENCIES AWAY FROM SELLING ON PRICE

Stop looking like the mass of undifferentiated competitors that you have. Otherwise you will only be able to compete on price.

And that is a mug's game!

It seems like a no-brainer that you need to be better than your competitors at (the word you hate) selling.

Your marketing needs to be more compelling and it needs to be different from the rest.

After all, why should I buy from you if you are the same as the competition?

With that in mind, and looking at successful marketing and digital agencies that we have been involved with over the years, we have compiled a manifesto – more than a white paper; almost an aspirational doctrine – to lead agencies away from selling on price.

A piece that is all about agencies!

THE MANIFESTO

We will not become a *'jack of all trades and master of none'*
> - we are a specialist with specialist expertise in a specialist subject. We are not just another general practitioner with the same general set of guiding principles as our competitors. That would be commercial suicide.

We don't do sales pitches
> - we have far less futile and humiliating things that we can do to win business. But we will talk. We like to talk to people and find out what they are really looking for and what they are really like. We want to make sure that there is a real fit between how we work best and what the client is looking for. We need to understand you and what your problem really is.

We are not suppliers
> - we are partners in the growth and development of our clients. Suppliers are ten-a-penny; they sell and compete on price and not on quality. That is not us.

We don't do endless freebies and beauty parades
> - while we are happy to do pro bono work for our chosen special causes, we do not and will not endlessly give away our intellectual property on a

gamble that you might think we might be able to deliver some more (but in likelihood you will steal our ideas or ask us to use the ideas you have stolen from others).

We don't get interviewed by you

- we will interview each other and make sure that the fit works for everyone. We will walk away if the chemistry and dynamics aren't working or if we don't believe that you believe in us.

We will make no recommendations

- unless we have done the initial audit, healthcheck or diagnostics. Would you trust a heart surgeon who didn't put you through all the diagnostic tests before making a recommendation to operate?

We will apply all aspects of 'The Expert'* model

- we will talk and write and deliver to a select audience with a specific set of problems. We have evidence and proof that we can address and resolve their issues. We have a proprietary point of view; we deliver wow work!

We will not compete on price

- being the cheapest is not our goal. It doesn't help the client and it doesn't help us if we cut corners or simply look for quick wins when fundamental, deep-seated change is required.

We will not sell time

    - we will deliver a value-added service and avoid charging by the hour or by the day. Clients are buying our years of experience, originality of our ideas and our ability to deliver. And we will walk away if we are not adding significant value to your business. How can you put a price on that?

We will talk money

    - we won't pray that no-one mentions budgets. We explicitly talk about money to make sure that we do not waste our time or yours. We know we deliver stunning added-value. We are not ashamed of our fees. They enable us to invest in delivering even better value.

We will define the overt business benefit of working with us, explicitly

    - we will explain the actual numbers of working with us

    eg *'our clients typically see a 30% uplift in profit within 90 days of working with us'*.

We will give a real reason to believe that we can deliver

    - evidence, proofs, testimonials, word-of-mouth reputation...

We will be dramatically different from the competition.

We will enjoy ourselves. Life is too short.

*For more on 'The Expert' model see my book, *Grow Your Service Firm.*

Download the Digital Agency Manifesto pdf from www.directorscentre.com/knowledgecentre

Bibliography, Further Reading

Armstrong, Michael   How to Be An Even More Effective Manager, Kogan Page, 1994

Baer, Jay   Youtility: Why Smart Marketing Is About Help Not Hype, Portfolio, 2013

Carroll, Lewis   Alice's Adventures In Wonderland, Collins, 2010

Burke G, Clarke L, Molian D & Barrow P   Growing Your Business, Routledge, 2008

Churchill NC & Lewis VL   The Five Stages Of Small Business Growth, HBR, 1993

Collis DJ & Rukstad MG   Can You Say What Your Strategy Is?, HBR, April 2008

Covey, Stephen   Seven Habits Of Highly Effective People, Simon & Schuster, 1999

Craven, Robert   Bright Marketing, Crimson Books, 2007

Craven, Robert	Customer Is King, Virgin Books, 2005
Craven, Robert	Grow Your Service Firm, Crimson Books, 2012
Craven, Robert	Kick-Start Your Business, Virgin Books, 2005
Craven, Robert	The Sales Funnel Is Dead, pdf, http://robert-craven.com/the-sales-funnel-is-dead-long-live-the-king/, 2014
Dixon M, Toman N, Delisi R	Effortless Experience, Portfolio, 2013
Ferriss, Tim	The 4-Hour Workweek, Crown Business, 2007
Gerber, Michael E	The E-Myth Manager, Harper Collins, 1999
Goldsmith, Marshall	What Got You Here Won't Get You There, Profile, 2008
Google	Zero Moment Of Truth (ZMOT), www.thinkwithgoogle.com/collecti ons/zero-moment-truth.html, 2014
Hall, Doug	Jump-Start Your Business Brain, Cherisey Press, 2004
Hsieh, Tony	Delivering Happiness: A Path To

	Profits. Passion, And Purpose, Business Plus, 2010
Inst. of Practitioners in Advertising	Advertising In A Downturn, IPA, 2008
Jones, Graham	Clickology: What Works In Online Shopping And How Your Business Can... N Brealey, 2014
Kaplan, RS & Norton DP	Strategy Maps: Converting Intangible Assets Into Tangible Outcomes, Harvard Business Press, 2003
Maister, David H	Managing The Professional Service Firm, Simon & Schuster, 1997
McDonald, M & Wilson, H	Marketing Plans: How To Prepare Them, How To Use Them, Wiley, 2011
Roetzer, Paul	The Marketing Agency Blueprint: The Handbook For Building Hybrid PR, SEO, Content, Advertising, And Web Firms, Wiley, 2011
Sinek, Simon	Leaders Eat Last: Why Some Teams Pull Together And Others Don't, Penguin, 2014
Vaynerchuck, Guy	Jab, Jab, Jab, Right Hook: How To Tell Your Story In A Noisy Social World, Harper Business, 2013

About The Author

Robert Craven works with ambitious owner-directors of fast-growing agencies and businesses who feel that they could be doing even better.

Robert set up the first of several businesses (restaurant, cafe, training company, sound studio) in his final year at university. He then spent five years running training and consultancy programmes for entrepreneurs at *Warwick Business School*. Running his own consultancy, The Directors' Centre, since 1998, he is now one of the UK's best-known speakers on growing your business.

Alongside numerous speaking engagements, Robert also does consulting work for, and is personal mentor to, a number of growing UK agencies and businesses.

He lives near Bath with his wife and three dogs - his three fabulous children have escaped to live their own lives!

Contact Details

E: rc@robert-craven.com
W: www.robert-craven.com
Twitter: @robert_craven
LinkedIn: www.linkedin.com/in/robertcraven
T: +44 (0)1225 851044

Also By The Author

Great British Entrepreneur's Handbook 2015*, Harriman House, 2015
Crunch Questions, Directors' Centre, 2013
Grow Your Service Firm, Crimson, 2012
Business Gurus*, Crimson, 2012
Bright Marketing For Small Business, Crimson, 2011
Beating The Credit Crunch, Directors' Centre, 2008
Bright Marketing: Why Should People…, Crimson, 2007
The Start-Up Essays, Directors' Centre, 2004
Customer Is King, Virgin, 2002/14
Kick-Start Your Business, Virgin, 2001/5

* co-author

The Directors' Centre

The **Directors' Centre** works with ambitious directors and owners of agencies and businesses who have concerns about the way their business is growing – they are growing too quickly or not quickly enough!

Clients work with us because we are challenging, honest and goading. Because we help them run the agency they really want to run.

The team knows how to grow a business - they have all been there and done it... ...which means that you get straightforward, no-nonsense solutions to your problems.

E:	office@directorscentre.com
W:	www.directorscentre.com
FaceBook:	http://www.facebook.com/directorscentre
T:	+44 (0)1225 851044

INDEX

42806424R00071

Made in the USA
Charleston, SC
05 June 2015